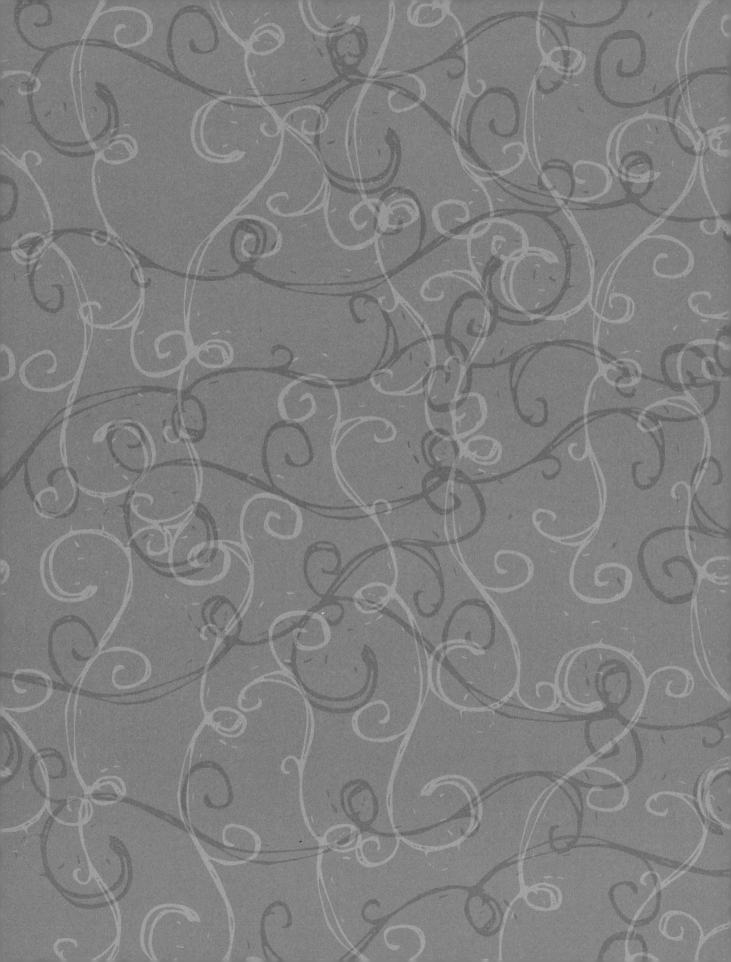

MORE ANIMAL FAIRY TALES

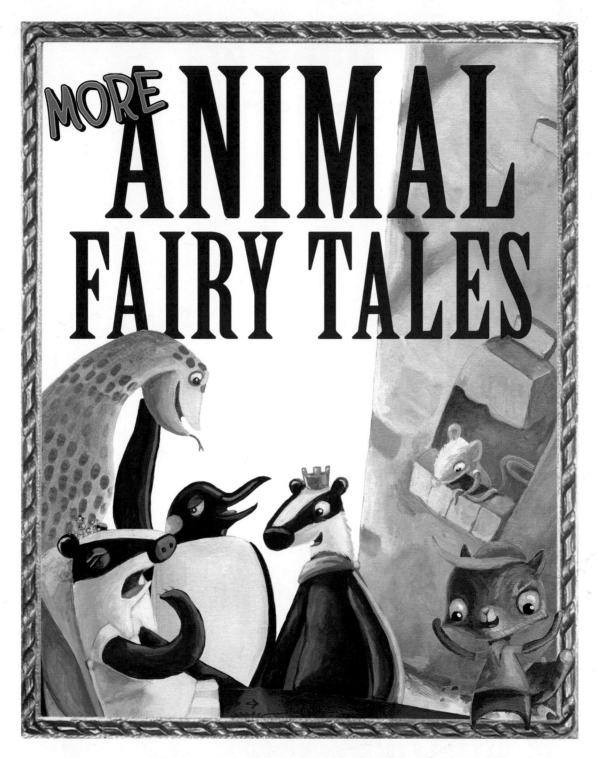

MORE ANIMAL FAIRY TALES

written by Charlotte Guillain ☆ illustrated by Dawn Beacon

Raintree

Chicago, Illinois

Table of Contents

Rumplesnakeskin

Characters

Sybil

 Sybil's Father

King

Rumplesnakeskin

 Prince

Once upon a time, there lived a beautiful squirrel named Sybil. Her father liked to boast about Sybil, telling everyone how wonderful she was. One day he even said that Sybil could turn acorns into gold!

Of course, it wasn't true! But when the king heard the story, he called Sybil to the palace and shut her in a room full of acorns.

"Turn the acorns into gold by morning or I will chop off your beautiful bushy tail," he ordered.

The king's son, a handsome prince, begged his father not to hurt Sybil.

Sybil sat on the floor and cried.
All of a sudden, a snake appeared
before her.

"Lissssten! I will turn the acornsssss
into gold if you give me your
necklace," he hissed. Sybil agreed.

In the morning, the room was full of golden acorns, and the king was very happy. But then he took Sybil to a bigger room, with an even bigger pile of acorns inside.

"Turn the acorns into gold by morning or I will chop off your beautiful bushy tail," the king demanded.

Again, Sybil sat on the floor and cried. But all of a sudden, the snake appeared again.

"Missssssss! I will turn the acornsssss into gold if you give me your ring," he hissed. Sybil agreed.

In the morning, the room was full of
golden acorns again. The king was
delighted. He took Sybil to an enormous
room filled with yet more acorns.

This time he said, "If you turn these acorns
into gold by morning you may marry my
son, the prince. But if you fail, I will chop
off your beautiful bushy tail."

Once more, Sybil sat on the floor and cried. Once more, the snake slithered into the room. But this time, Sybil had nothing left to give him.

"I will turn the acornsssss into gold if you promisssse to give me your first baby sssssquirrel," said the snake slyly. Sybil sadly agreed.

In the morning, the room was full of golden acorns. Sybil and the prince were married. But when a baby was born, the snake returned.

Sybil begged him not to take her baby. "You have three chancessss to guesssss my name," hissed the snake. "If you guesssss correctly, you can keep your baby."

On the following two mornings, Sybil tried to guess the snake's name, but she was wrong both times.

On the third morning, Sybil heard the snake singing outside.
He sang, "She'll never win this guesssssing game, Rumplessssnakeskin is my name!"

Sybil hid her excitement as the snake slithered in.

"One more guesssss," he hissed.

"Um...is your name...Rumplesnakeskin?" asked Sybil.

The snake gave a hiss of rage! He was so angry that his skin split in two and he hurried away, leaving just his snakeskin behind. And Sybil, the prince, and their baby lived happily ever after.

The End

Where does this story come from?

You've probably already heard the story that *Rumplesnakeskin* is based on—*Rumplestiltskin*. There are many different versions of this story. When people tell a story, they often make little changes to make it their own. How would you change this story?

◦◦◦◦◦◦◦◦◦◦

The history of the story

Rumplestiltskin was first written down by the Brothers Grimm. Jacob (1785–1863) and Wilhelm (1786–1859) Grimm lived near the city of Frankfurt, in Germany. They collected and wrote down many fairy stories and folktales. These tales were told by storytellers who entertained people in the days before radio and television.

In the original story, a miller boasts to the king about his daughter, claiming that she can spin straw into gold. The king shuts the daughter away in a tower filled with straw and a spinning wheel. He tells her to spin the straw into gold by morning or he will chop off her head. The girl despairs, but then a strange creature appears and offers to spin the straw into gold in return for the girl's necklace. In the morning, the king takes the girl to an even bigger room, full of more straw. The creature appears again and helps the girl in return for her ring. On the third day, the girl is shut in an even bigger room full of straw, but this time she has nothing to give the creature in return for his help. In the end, she promises her firstborn child to him if he will spin the straw into gold again. In the morning, the girl is released. She marries the king and becomes queen. But when she has a child, the creature reappears and demands that she keep her promise. When she begs for mercy, he gives her three chances to guess his name—if she guesses correctly she can keep her baby. He comes back the next two mornings, but the queen cannot guess his name. On the final night, the queen's messenger is riding through the forest when he hears the creature singing a song that includes his name. The messenger passes this on to the queen, who is able to tell the creature what his name is on the third morning. Rumplestiltskin leaves empty-handed in a rage, and the queen lives happily ever after.

The Emperor Penguin's New Clothes

Characters

Emperor Penguin

Penguin Servant

Killer Whale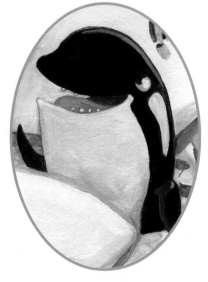

 Subjects

There was once a snowy land that was ruled by Emperor Penguin.

Every morning he would stand on a hill to look down at all the other penguins and feel very important.

One day Emperor Penguin was watching all the other penguins on the ice when Killer Whale popped up out of the sea and looked at him.

"You look very important," said Killer Whale.

"Oh, I am," said Emperor Penguin snootily. "I am the emperor of all penguins. I am much more special than all these other penguins."

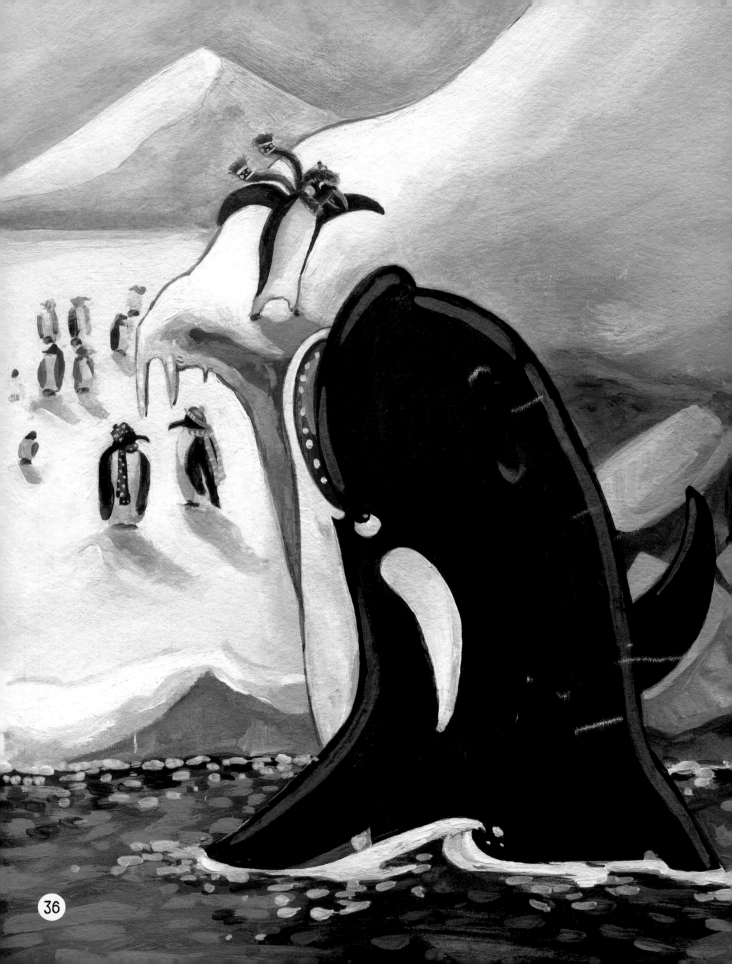

Killer Whale looked around and sighed.
"It's a shame. You look just the same
as all these other penguins," he said.

"Someone as important as you
should surely look different from
everyone else."

Emperor Penguin was shocked.
"You're right!" he said. "Everyone
should see that I am more special
than other penguins."

"I will help you," said Killer Whale.
"Bring me a thousand fish, and I will
make you look special."

So Emperor Penguin made his servants
catch one thousand fish and take them
to Killer Whale. Then Killer Whale
gobbled up the fish, and he looked at
the emperor.

"This is what you need to do," he whispered in Emperor Penguin's ear.

The next morning, all the penguins woke
up and went about their business. As usual,
Emperor Penguin took his place standing
on the hill looking down on everyone.

"Um, your majesty," said a nervous servant, "You've forgotten to put on your clothes!"

"Ha!" scoffed Emperor Penguin.
"You fool! I'm wearing a special suit
that Killer Whale gave me. He told
me that it would be invisible to foolish,
ordinary penguins."

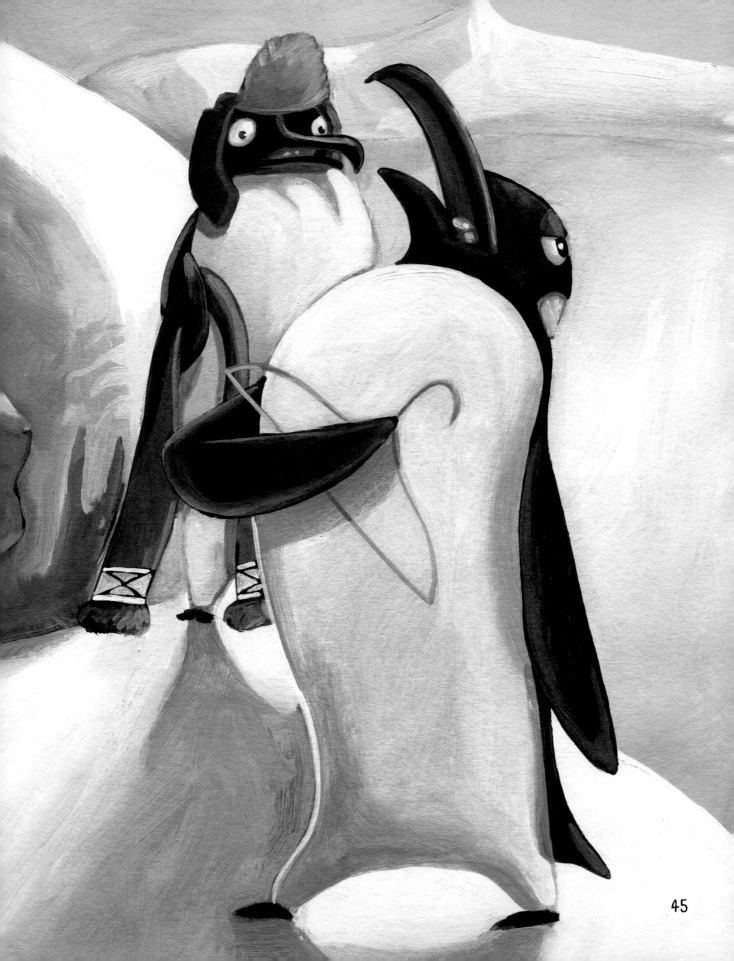

Emperor Penguin paraded across
the ice, proudly declaring, "See how
important I am? My new suit is so
special that only I can see it!"
The other penguins watched him
pass by as he started to shiver.

A small penguin chick shouted,
"Look at that silly penguin! He's
forgotten to put on his clothes!"

All the other penguins laughed, and
Emperor Penguin realized how foolish
he had been. From that day on, he wore
warm clothes like the other penguins. And
he never listened to Killer Whale again!

The End

Where does this story come from?

You've probably already heard the story that *The Emperor Penguin's New Clothes* is based on—*The Emperor's New Clothes*. There are many different versions of this story. When people tell a story, they often make little changes to make it their own. How would you change this story?

⌒⌒⌒ ⋅ ⌒⌒⌒

The history of the story

The Emperor's New Clothes was written by Hans Christian Andersen. Andersen was born in 1805 and lived in Denmark. He wrote many poems and stories, including many fairy tales. Andersen's fairy stories became famous around the world.

In the original story, a foolish, vain emperor is tricked by two weavers. They sell him a suit of fine clothes that they claim is only visible to the most important and intelligent people. The emperor can't see anything, but he doesn't want to be thought of as unimportant or stupid. He claims that he loves the suit and allows the weavers to "dress" him in it. When he goes out wearing nothing, everyone is too scared to say anything, even though he is naked. Finally, a small child says what everyone is thinking, and the emperor is shown to be a fool.

Sleeping Badger

Characters

Bella Badger

 King and Queen

Fairy Godmothers

Wicked Wasp

Prince Snuffling

Once upon a time, a happy king and queen lived in a palace deep in the forest. Their happiness was complete when a baby princess was born. They named her Bella and held a big party to celebrate.

It's a Girl!

The king and queen invited three magic butterflies to be their daughter's fairy godmothers. Each godmother brought a special gift for Princess Bella.

The first godmother gave the baby the
gift of intelligence and fun. The second
gave the gift of beauty and music.
The third godmother was about to give
her gift when a shadow fell over
the room.

A wicked wasp flew in. She was mad that she had not been invited to the party. "I put this baby under a spell," the wasp buzzed angrily. "She will be stung by a wasp and die before her 16th birthday."

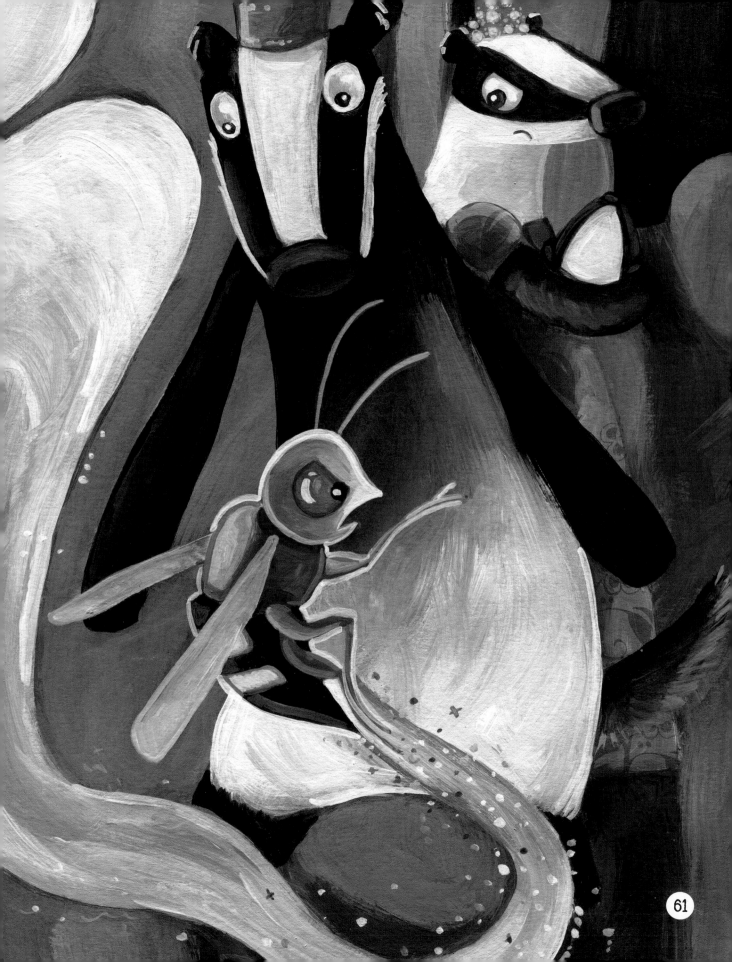

61

The wasp flew away, laughing. The last butterfly godmother thought quickly before she gave her gift to the baby.

"I cannot stop the wasp's spell," she said. "But if Bella is stung, she will not die. Instead she will sleep for 100 years and will only be woken up by a kiss from a prince."

The years passed and Bella grew up.
Everyone in the palace made sure that
no wasps ever came near her.

As her 16th birthday approached,
the king and queen hoped that Bella
might escape the wasp's spell.

But the day before her 16th birthday, Bella heard a buzzing sound outside. She went out to explore and saw a juicy apple. She did not see the wasp hiding behind it. As Bella reached out to take the apple, the wasp stung her, and she fell asleep.

The king and queen were horrified.
They carried the sleeping Bella back
to her room. When the butterfly
godmothers saw how upset the king
and queen were, they magically put
everyone in the castle to sleep, too.

One hundred years passed and thorny
bushes grew around the sleeping palace.
One day, Prince Snuffling was passing
through the forest when he spotted the
palace behind the thick brambles. He cut
his way through and went inside, where
he found the sleeping princess.

Prince Snuffling thought Bella was beautiful! He gave her a kiss, and she began to wake up. Then everyone else in the palace began to stir. They were delighted to see Bella waking up.

It was not long before another party was held in the palace—for Bella and Prince Snuffling's wedding. And they all lived happily ever after.

The End

Where does this story come from?

You've probably already heard the story that *Sleeping Badger* is based on—*Sleeping Beauty*. There are many different versions of this story. When people tell a story, they often make little changes to make it their own. How would you change this story?

The history of the story

Sleeping Beauty was first written by Charles Perrault in a collection of fairy tales in 1697. Charles Perrault collected popular folktales and created the first written fairy tales. Later the Brothers Grimm, from Germany, rewrote several of these stories.

In the original tale, a king and queen invite seven fairy godmothers to their daughter's christening. They begin to give the baby their gifts when they are interrupted by a wicked fairy who casts a spell on the princess, saying she will be pricked by a spindle and die. The last good fairy tries to counteract this spell by casting her own—the princess will instead fall asleep for 100 years and be woken up by a prince's kiss. Despite everyone's efforts, the princess is pricked by a spindle and falls asleep. The seventh fairy then puts everyone else asleep because they are so upset. She also makes thorns grow around the palace to protect the sleeping princess. After 100 years, a prince finds the palace and wakes up Sleeping Beauty. The spell is broken, and everyone lives happily ever after.

Cat and the Beanstalk

Characters

Cat

Giant Dog

Cat's Mother

Old Weasel

There was once a young kitten named Cat who lived with his mother. They were very poor.

One day, things had gotten so bad that Cat's mother sent him to the market to sell their cat basket.

On the way to the market, Cat met an
old weasel.

"Where are you going?" asked the weasel.

"I'm going to the market to sell our cat
basket," replied Cat.

"I'll give you three magic beans for your
cat basket," said the weasel. Cat agreed
and hurried home to show the beans to
his mother.

But Cat's mother was very angry
when she saw the magic beans. She
threw them out of the window. Cat
and his mother went to sleep feeling
hungry and uncomfortable without
any food or their basket.

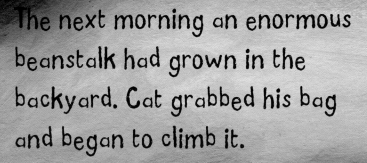

The next morning an enormous
beanstalk had grown in the
backyard. Cat grabbed his bag
and began to climb it.

At the top of the beanstalk, Cat found himself in a strange land where everything was enormous.

He sneaked inside a huge castle to look around. He came across a room full of golden cans of pet food!

Cat could hear loud snoring. He crept farther into the room. In the corner, a giant dog was fast asleep. Cat filled his bag with pet food and tiptoed away. He climbed back down the beanstalk.

Cat's mother was very happy when she
saw the golden cans.
"Go back up tomorrow and see what
else you can find," she told him.

So the next morning, Cat climbed up
the beanstalk again. He sneaked back
into the giant dog's room in the castle.

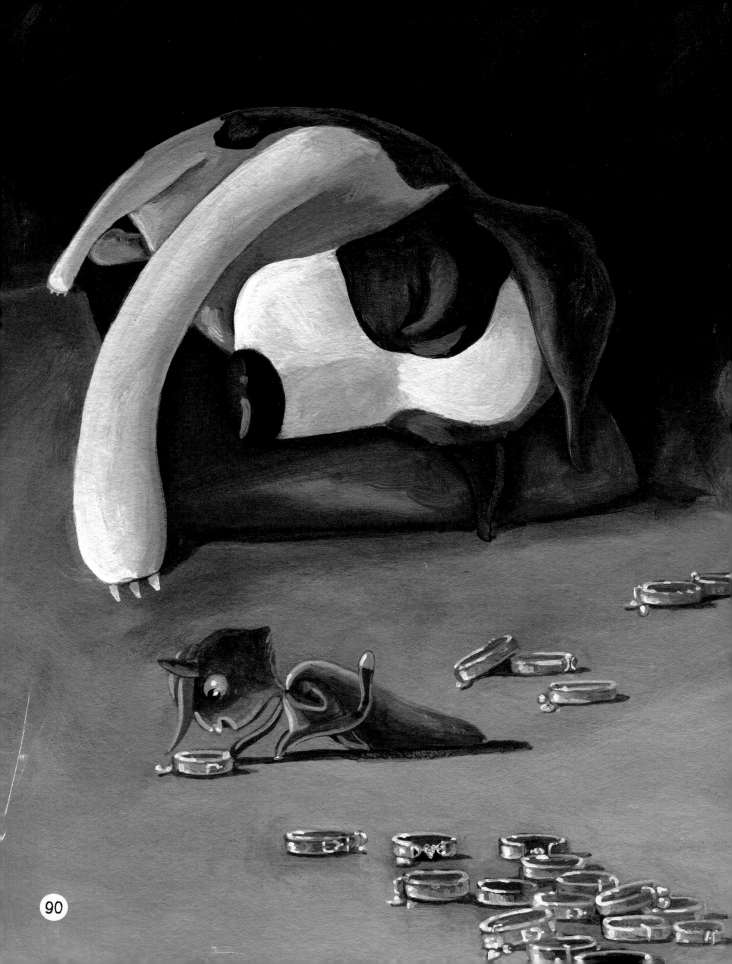

This time, Cat found a pile of glittering golden pet collars! Cat could hear the giant dog snoring again, but he picked up the collars and tiptoed away without waking him.

Cat climbed back down the beanstalk, and his mother was delighted with the golden collars.

The next morning, Cat's mother was
pointing at the beanstalk again.
"Go back up and see what else you can
find!" she said.

So Cat climbed back up the beanstalk and
sneaked back into the castle. In the giant
dog's room was a pile of magic pet toys.
As the dog snored, Cat filled his bag and
started to tiptoe away.

Cat crept to the top of the beanstalk and
was about to climb down when the golden
toys in his bag started to rattle! Cat froze
as he heard the sound of the giant dog
barking from the castle.

"Fee-fi-fo-fat,
I smell the blood of a furry cat!
Be he orange or striped or black,
I'll eat him for my morning snack!"

Cat heard the giant dog running after him. He hurried down the beanstalk, with the toys rattling loudly in his bag. When Cat got to the bottom, he grabbed an ax and chopped the beanstalk down. He was safe!

Cat and his mother were rich. They lived happily ever after, and Cat never had to go on an adventure ever again.

The End

Where does this story come from?

You've probably already heard the story that *Cat and the Beanstalk* is based on—*Jack and the Beanstalk*. There are many different versions of this story. When people tell a story, they often make little changes to make it their own. How would you change this story?

The history of the story

Jack and the Beanstalk is an English folktale that was told by oral storytellers for many years before it was written down. Storytellers entertained people in the days before radio and television. The story was written down in various collections, such as Joseph Jacobs's *English Fairy Tales* in 1890.

The original story tells of a young boy, Jack, who lives with his mother, who is a widow. They are very poor. When their cow stops providing them with milk, Jack's mother sends him to the market to sell the animal. On the way to the market, an old man gives Jack some magic beans for the cow, but Jack's mother is furious when he returns home without any money. She throws the beans out of the window and sends Jack to bed. Overnight a giant beanstalk grows, and in the morning Jack climbs it. At the top is a strange land where a giant lives. The giant's wife gives Jack some food, but when the giant smells him, Jack has to hide to avoid being eaten. He steals a bag of gold and escapes down the beanstalk. Jack returns two more times and is helped by the giant's wife before he steals a hen that lays golden eggs, and then a magic harp. When he steals the harp, it plays music and alerts the giant, who almost catches Jack. Then Jack escapes by chopping down the beanstalk and killing the giant. Jack and his mother live happily ever after and are never poor again.

Ratpunzel

Characters

Ratpunzel

Mother and Father

Cruel Cat

Prince Ratdolph

Once upon a time, there were two rats
who loved each other very much.
One day the wife became sick.

"Please fetch some special seeds from
the forest for me to eat," she begged
her husband. He did as she asked for
two nights, and she began to get better.

On the third night, the husband went
back to the forest to fetch more seeds,
but he was caught by a cruel cat.
He begged for mercy.

"I will let you go if you promise to give me your first baby," purred the cat. Terrified, the husband agreed and scurried away.

Time passed and the couple had
a baby daughter.
They named her Ratpunzel.

One morning the cat appeared.
"You must keep your promise and
give me the child," said the cat,
taking Ratpunzel away.

Ratpunzel grew up into a beautiful rat, with a very long tail. The cat hid Ratpunzel away in a tall tower, deep in the forest.

Only the cat could visit her, by climbing up Ratpunzel's tail.

Ratpunzel had a beautiful voice, and
she would spend her time singing
at the top of the tower. One day,
handsome Prince Ratdolph was riding
through the forest.

Prince Ratdolph heard Ratpunzel
singing. He followed the sound and saw
the cat climbing up Ratpunzel's tail.

Prince Ratdolph came back that night.
"Let down your tail!" he called like
the cat. Ratpunzel did as he asked, and
Prince Ratdolph climbed up into the tower.

Prince Ratdolph and Ratpunzel fell in
love. He visited her every night, taking
thread for Ratpunzel to weave into a
ladder to escape.

Time passed and Ratpunzel had almost finished weaving the ladder for her escape.

One morning the cat came to visit her. "You're so much heavier to pull up than the prince," puffed Ratpunzel.

The cat was furious that Prince Ratdolph had visited. He sent Ratpunzel out into the forest.

That night, Prince Ratdolph came to see Ratpunzel as usual. The cat pulled him up by using a rope.

"You will never see Ratpunzel again!" he snarled when the prince reached the top of the tower. The prince jumped from the tower to escape.

Prince Ratdolph landed in a thornbush, which scratched his eyes and blinded him. He wandered in the deep, dark forest day and night, unable to see.

But one day he heard
a familiar voice
singing beautifully.

Prince Ratdolph followed the voice into a clearing, where he fell into Ratpunzel's paws. She wept when she saw his scratched eyes. Magically, her tears brought his sight back.

Prince Ratdolph and Ratpunzel were married and lived happily ever after.

The End

Where does this story come from?

You've probably already heard the story that *Ratpunzel* is based on—*Rapunzel*. There are many different versions of this story. When people tell a story, they often make little changes to make it their own. How would you change this story?

The history of the story

Rapunzel was first written down by the Brothers Grimm. Jacob (1785–1863) and Wilhelm (1786–1859) Grimm lived near the city of Frankfurt, in Germany. They collected and wrote down many fairy stories and folktales. These tales were told by storytellers who entertained people in the days before radio and television.

In the original story, a husband and wife live next to a witch. The wife is pregnant and craves a plant called rapunzel from the witch's garden, so her husband goes to fetch it for her. But on the third night, the witch catches him and makes him promise her his unborn child. The promise is kept, and the witch names the baby Rapunzel. The girl grows up to be beautiful with long golden hair, so the witch hides her away in a tall tower with no door or stairs. Only the witch can enter the tower by climbing Rapunzel's hair. A prince hears Rapunzel singing and learns how to climb up to see her. They fall in love and plan Rapunzel's escape, but she accidentally gives the plan away to the witch. The witch cuts off Rapunzel's hair and casts her out into the forest. When the prince visits, the witch lets down Rapunzel's cut hair and pulls him up into the tower. When he discovers what has happened, he jumps from the tower and is blinded by a thornbush. As he wanders through the forest, he eventually hears Rapunzel singing and they are reunited. Her loving tears restore his sight, and they live happily ever after.

About the author

Charlotte Guillain has written nearly 100 books,
both fiction and nonfiction. Before writing children's books,
Charlotte worked as a bookseller, a teacher of
English as a foreign language, and an editor.

About the illustrator

Dawn Beacon lives with her husband and son
in the beautiful mountains of Colorado. Inspiration for
her artwork is found directly outside her back door,
in the abundance of wildlife and breathtaking
views of her surroundings.

© 2014 Raintree
an imprint of Capstone Global Library, LLC
Chicago, Illinois

To contact Capstone Global Library please call 800-747-4992, or visit
our web site: www.capstoneyoungreaders.com

Library of Congress Cataloging-in-Publication Data is available
on the Library of Congress website.
ISBN: 978-1-4109-6784-8

Edited by Daniel Nunn, Rebecca Rissman, and Catherine Veitch
Designed by Joanna Hinton-Malivoire
Original illustrations © Capstone Global Library, Ltd, 2014
Illustrated by Dawn Beacon
Production by Victoria Fitzgerald
Originated by Capstone Global Library, Ltd

Printed and bound in China.
012014   007983

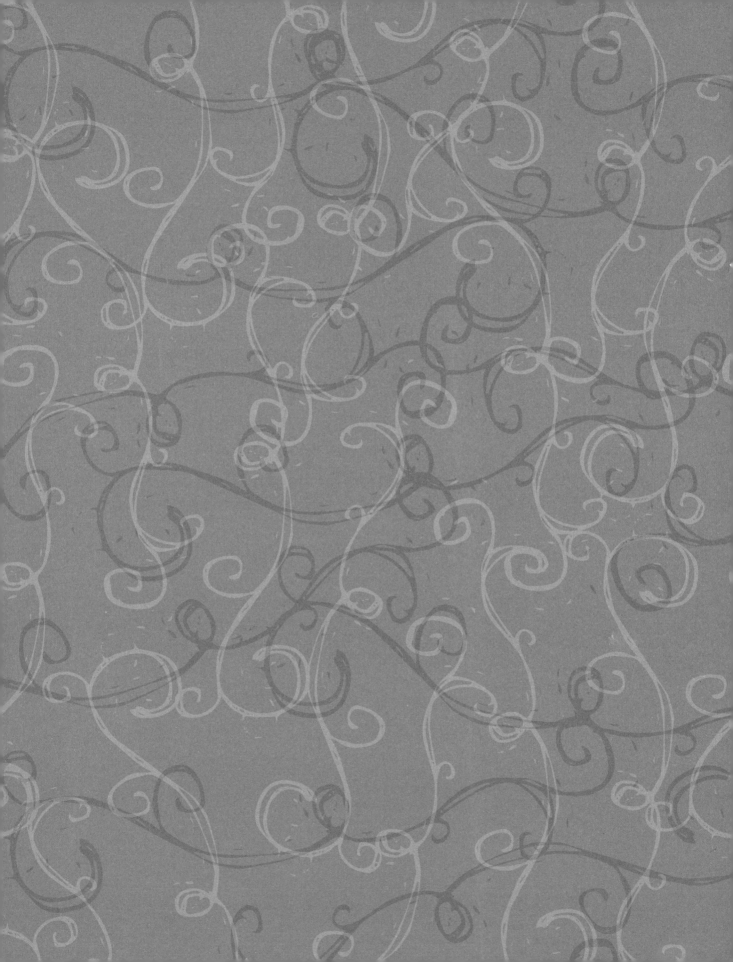

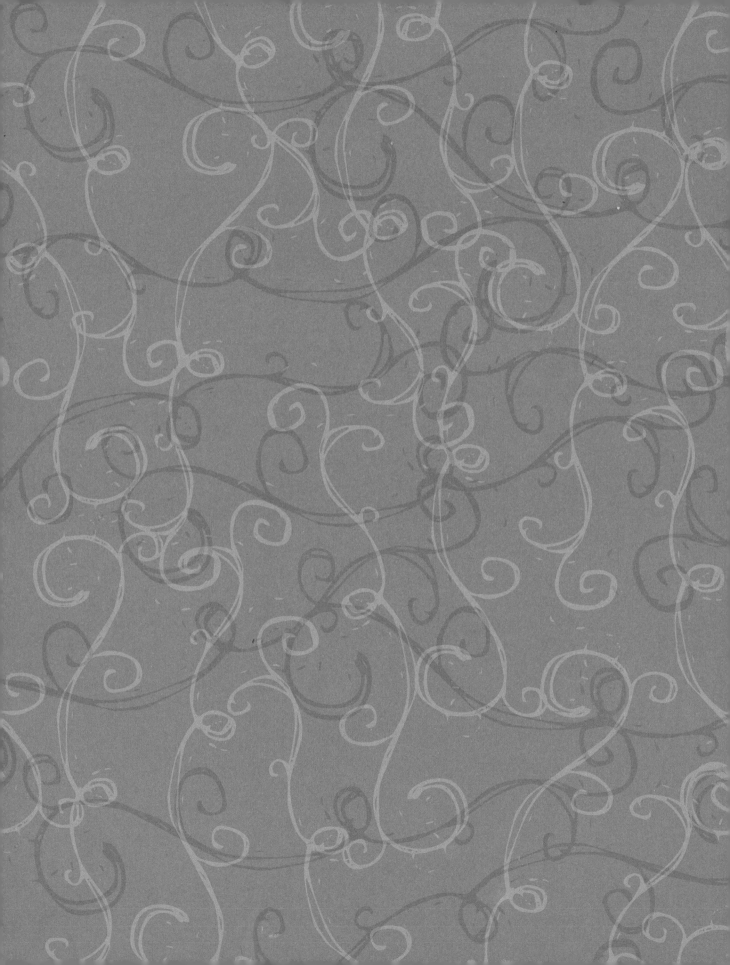